Divers

Cover art: "Batterman Dives (Multiflash), 1955" © Harold Edgerton/MIT, courtesy Palm Press, Inc.
Cover typeface: Abril Fatface

Interior design by Laura Joakimson
Interior typeface: Garamond Premier Pro

Library of Congress Cataloging-in-Publication Data

Names: Amadon, Samuel author
Title: Divers / Samuel Charles Amadon.
Description: Oakland, California : Omnidawn Publishing, 2026. | Summary: "This book-length sequence of turbulent sonnets follows their speaker's impulses and imagination through the seasons of their composition. These poems are rigorously constrained while also making space for improvisation. They hold to a decasyllabic line while moving in and out of meter. They sing of time, and struggle to understand it. They find words for our moment in the pages of old books. Lines from great writers of the past--including Gerard Manley Hopkins, Thomas Wyatt, and Michael Drayton--echo through Amadon's poems of contemporary menace and wonder. Here we see both the owls lining our fences and the black SUVs rolling down our streets. Out of these conflicts, Amadon's sonnets step up, lift off, and dive into themselves"-- Provided by publisher.

Identifiers: LCCN 2026020706 (print) | LCCN 2026020707 (ebook) | ISBN 9781632432254 trade paperback | ISBN 9781632432315 epub
Subjects: LCGFT: Sonnets
Classification: LCC PS3601.M33 D58 2026 (print) | LCC PS3601.M33 (ebook) | DDC 811/.6--dc23/eng/20260416
LC record available at https://lccn.loc.gov/2026020706
LC ebook record available at https://lccn.loc.gov/2026020707

Published by Omnidawn Publishing, Oakland, California
www.omnidawn.com
10 9 8 7 6 5 4 3 2 1
ISBN: 978-1-63243-225-4

I love this book. Assured and expansive, Samuel Amadon's sonnets achieve an exquisite balance of rigor and ease. Each poem drops the reader into a mind where inner climate and outer climate are often indistinguishable, and where weather becomes both subject and method. Attentive, embodied, and turning with the turning of seasons, these sonnets are alive to the conditions that make thought itself possible, issuing an invitation to fall in love with living again and again.
—Cecily Parks, author of *The Seeds*

Samuel Amadon's *Divers* offers a scintillating collection of sonnets that breathe as fluidly as flutes in a cathedral foyer. Through a Whitmanian musicality pulsing with intellectual curiosity, tuned to the organic world's quiet rhythms and inner weather, each poem acts as a station for language and consciousness modulating each other into a higher order of understanding. The result is a world dis-alienating poetry that thinks with the world, instead of about it.
—Rodrigo Toscano, author of *WHITMAN. CANNONBALL. PUEBLA.*

For centuries, the sonnet has provided the joy of exuberance within the constraints of received form, and Samuel Amadon's *Divers* extends the tradition of the art into a world that is familiar but, in his hands, is also newly strange. With language that is spiked with an intoxicating spirit, Amadon's new work is both stimulant and balm.
—Mark Wunderlich, author of *God of Nothingness*

also by Samuel Amadon

Often, Common, Some, and Free, Omnidawn Publishing, 2021

Listener, Solid Objects, 2020

The Hartford Book, Cleveland State University Poetry Center, 2012

Like a Sea, University of Iowa Press, 2010

Divers

Samuel Amadon

OMNIDAWN PUBLISHING
OAKLAND, CALIFORNIA
2026

For Liz Countryman

The king is dead.

—Marianne Moore

TABLE OF CONTENTS

///

////

/ // /// //// /////

(I)

Oh Monday, I said I had to look at
You and live with it. Oh your face is full
Of holes I could put through each my eyes.
They'd be blue swoops, pretty diagonals
I could form from moving things around me.
Whatever you do, Monday, I can't tell
The difference. How do I order you?
I cut a bag three holes to make a face,
And what was me vanishes like wind through
A skull. If I know what I want to say,
I find I can't speak straight. On the windows,
April accumulates. I mouth my eyes
Are gray, plain. I make nothing behave
As pollinated rains curl down the drain.

(II)

A spring thought. I put it down where I stood,
While I shut the window on a housefly.
The garden beds are full of them, compost
Sweet as words with all their meanings. I tried
My back against the wall. I tried my knee
There on the chair. I felt as if my voice
Echoed if I spoke, like a corridor
Filled with mall voices. Here, where there's nothing
But color flattening into its shades.
Silver gray slate then red. I expected
A flower as I brought it closer, but
That wasn't what it was, like opening
The door on the porch to find the gray day
Has turned blue, unending and overdue.

(III)

I see myself as I truly behave.
Searching each room for a sound, a humming
I feel discontent with. Each of these days
I wanted to make my own cardboard,
And I wanted to think about cardboard,
No, not to touch it, not to order it
Into place, but to be covered over
With it without contact, like hovering
Inside an egg. Inside a scent, yellow
As a glimmer or the path it makes on
A yellow wall as someone's watch face moves
Around the room. It was a certain time
Of day. It was the midst of a season.
Each moment as alterable as clay.

(IV)

I love the trees when they are patient. Here,
In a world filled up with places, I plot,
And my head fills me in with what I've planned.
I more more do and spit. I spit. I spit
On the concrete while blue. I find these words
Real beautiful. I use them over
The porch green and sweet and orange and then
Everything red in my car again.
Oh a car-made wind takes me now I'm young.
Breathing, my place is full of breath, and as
A springtime month folds out my chest, words fall
Down and around like hair in wind, while I
Circle a parking lot. I'm caught. I breeze
And blur and won't pull into any spot.

(V)

There are many things overhead. Grand things
Overhead, revolving, open, and fanned
Like surfaces, air, the sky flattened wide
With sunlight, which hits upon my seat. See,
I am casual. I don't interact
With each thought I spot. I get work in dirt.
I pull grasses weeds under bloom bloom trees.
A world curled so green and sweet for me. Thus,
I lose the sun in winds that drift and tilt
Above. I breathe in the towering air,
And tomorrow the breeze is what I breathe
In me. Where I put my breath. I say where
I put my eyes my work is done. I roll
My body into garden holes I've dug.

(VI)

Today the words I find around are fields
I walk at the edge of then out into
As a storm blooms in from the mountain clouds.
And if I breathe with this rain, while flowers
Are flooded with my sight, then I love them
Like I love a pile of earth, like I love
Whatever colors one finds in a field.
I get heavy with them. A big blue lung.
And if I breathe, as the wind rises up,
Then a green rush can come out the ends of
What I imagine, something inside me
That wants to coil, though I don't think it
Will hold, when I don't know how to tell what
I said from what I saw in the soil.

(VII)

Like a dapple-dawn-drawn falcon, I wind
And ride over sweeping hills, garden green
Or asphalt curved, hills of thick weeds, where I,
High there in the sky, am pleased to gather
Petals unreal, petals a fantasy
I wake in the heart of—it is morning
Under my feet, out on the street, where I've
Nowhere to go nor anyone to meet.
Or I wake in air spread wide. The terrain
Portions of me floating down on red clay
Canyon walls, where gray gases circle
Bright particles underground to rivers,
Live and wild as office building lobbies
Tunneling voices to a herd of birds.

(VIII)

A blue and white rain fell on the plaza
Like a ghost opened its mouth and urged me,
Take shelter. I ran under the roof slats,
Over the concrete wheelstops. I felt weak.
I wanted my finger in earthy weeds—
A hummingbird sipping at the feeder.
But the days get harder, start to seem like
A wind blown out a parking lot city.
The story I told before, I told that.
No one said not to. I felt however
I wanted. It was awful, like a dream
Where the future brings the past back warm,
Leftover. Breathing out again, I had
A thought like rain across a field I fled.

(IX)

I had a feeling on the face of it
A song. In the yard, grasses in the wind,
Passing like the sun every morning,
Every morning with the last coffee
In the cup, cool like an acid, it swirled
In me, woke what was left where I was it
Leaving. I had a feeling flutter trees
On the face it stops. It stopped in me.
I had a feeling alright, a breeze in
The tree branches brought to me news of new
Shadows. A feeling the grasses sat tip
On end. It was an end. I lay wasted
All morning, as the afternoon arranged
An evening round my face in the blades.

(X)

And in the light it smelled a little of
Apples—there were flowers, pink and yellow
To glance at, to glance over at, briefly
To see, while every green collected in
A window before where I hung my head
In a half-happy stare. I was what there
Was to see, at least that's what I thought as
I sang anew. In my glare, I withdrew
Myself from the departure of the day.
This vision I had had turned fierce, and brought
Me more my window, and changed my view.
I saw great machines twist in what had been
The distance. Earth was moved, and the sky lit
Up with silver thoughts. None of them I knew.

(XI)

for Lucie Brock-Broido

A rod runs through something like me, I find,
Deep in the Georgia pine, while your news gets
Into my french fries on I-95,
Where I ask whether hills will look as blue
When we cannot talk anymore. I've cut
In where I see myself disappearing
Like a bridge flat in the grass bites into
The me and you of here. A gravity.
There are more things I've heard you someone say,
Weaving our eyes, wreathing round our bodies.
The hum of things which are alive and stay
That way. That we be by habit aloft
So then in ourselves, we escape the sea,
A light perceived about us as we leave.

(XII)

I woke up again where I had been. This
A first day or a last day of something.
I forgot everything I wanted
As music from the windows of passing
Cars raged then rang itself away. Not me,
I turned some shades in their shadows. I was
Overgrown. I clipped my belt and pulled it
Close. I stood in the rain until I
Fell. I was the creature of an hour.
Then the hour passed, but my time wasn't done.
I thought it best to leave it off, let it
Rest as I rolled myself from hedge to hedge.
The spring is come when birds are building nests.
I leave what I want, and I take what's left.

(XIII)

I find I am found in the middle of thoughts
I would not expect to find in me. Still,
My eyes are mine, my hands as well, and I
Keep them with me as I say some sentence
Dies inside. Yet, if I imagine life,
I find I'm alive, in sudden rushes
Of spring wind through car windows, where behind
My breathing a teenage feeling ends. Then,
A teenage feeling back across my skin.
Everywhere I go things settle in
Me—as I look back on now as if it's
My invention, as if in these thoughts is
What I catch not where I'm caught, as I sing,
And the songs I know aren't words I lost.

(XIV)

I like the indifferences, like things
With a little twitch in their hip, prayers
Left on the air. Something I could have been
Screening for keeps finding me my eyes in
What's underneath. So I nod I think at
What was right in what I said, as I grip
My seat, as everything returns to me
When I am afraid. A storm looms. I am
Prepared to plummet, to rephrase plummet
So as to be ordinary, a thing
Some me returned to earth as—a wind I
Hear puts me on edge. I like what I know.
My head in a book I already read.
I like the thingness of things passed unsaid.

/ // /// //// /////

(XV)

Summer speaks, as flowers bleed my teeth
Bright with colors. I know, or I like, which
Flowers I find on my feet, edging up
My face, between my fingers, in pockets,
Sleeves, car mirrors, coming out the air in
The wind I meet. I know I'm on a hill.
I like deliberately. My face shines
Florally. I notice things. There's no room
Left for the wind. It is a windless day.
Around me, preferences leisurely ease.
The grassy gnats flee. The rain won't come or
Leave. And here, a feeling curling finger
Around my ear closer than I can bear,
A fell season, while it whispers in me.

(XVI)

Ere thou be as tree bark grown through chainlink.
Ere thou be as black tint lowering glass
Idle in the night. Ere thou be as paths
The leaf branches open, doorways, through to
Boulder trees, needle beds, soft as bench seats.
Ere thou be as bicycle tire flattened
Sidewalk counted coins, a grape soda can
Rolling down video store aisles. Ere thou
Be as the other side of memories
Found in the heat, found for what loses them
Again, loses me, and my living out
This way. Ere thou be as sweet as hot wind.
Ere thou be as still in my seat, too worn
To rise eyes from the where and here of now.

(XVII)

My heart escapes me I don't know what to
Say. I don't collapse into the summer
Pollen settled on the paint of my porch
Swing slats. I sit straight, settle my belly,
A bell in the air. Blue worlds hang before
My eyes, a blue universe, its thickness
I stir lengthily with a breath I breathe.
A desire plucks me from this state, wild air
Catches me in my eye like flowerpots
Falling out of windows. The days line up
In a long thin row until I lose place,
And if I can't keep count, it all rounds down
To a horn sounding blocks away. Unsure,
As fingers fitting fingers in a form.

(XVIII)

Something illegible, like a storm cloud
In the far corner of my view, late June's
Heat, a dark breeze hazing between blades of
Darker lawns. July fingertips into
Several squares at the screen porch screen, eyes
Piling container ships with citrus peels,
August swirling behind peninsulas.
Everything at a distance. Then, here,
A lot of rain. September towering
Its waters in the center of the grass.
Crackling interference, the sun
Comes out while the moisture hangs in the yard.
Something further to the middle of things
Like there, where no month's name may lift the air.

(XIX)

As green as lawns line up in the morning,
As mist lifts an order into place, cars
Curve out of driveways in quiet arcs
Over blacktop, as distance holds between
Porch and porch, then porch and sidewalk, street,
Where there is movement, where clothes fit over
Skin, coolly, firm, in this favored hour,
Where a feeling comes together as it
Diminishes. A plan empties itself.
Content as a pocketful of cash slips
In pieces, anonymous, and never
Home. A walk away or toward the store.
The day turns around on the day too long.
A plain song colors the way and is gone.

(XX)

I don't give a fuck. Let the rain govern
Me. My hands and feet in the mud or perched
Atop a pile as I fall off of me.
I'm mulch. I see myself like I matter.
I am a being quiet as a nun,
How I seem seeming, how I seem one
Who knows the name of which wind fills his lungs.
The broad sun sinks down to tranquility.
The day ends. I put my bird to flower,
And leave the grass its fevers, holding no
Form, my gentleness is out on the sea,
As I settle sightless into myself,
I let nothing go—I am calm and free—
Angry as the wind I breathe out and in.

(XXI)

I'm waiting for someone to step in here
And shoot me in the head. I feel this in
My chest. Now, as I am reading, the breeze
Picks up, and I feel the chill of someone
Across my skin. If I moved my body
Into sun over grass, I would not be
Alone. An uncomfortable sentence
Is where I live on the edge of something.
Or not. The song changes. It is as if
I walked a steep hill. I'm breathing again.
I'm pouring myself a white pint of milk,
Which I will hold in my one hand, dinner
In the other, as I look for a tune
To sing out while I swallow and consume.

(XXII)

The dangled grapes will rot. I'll pull my voice
Out, while I play through what I have to say.
The storm will end. The ships will return. And
I will know what I want to talk about
When we get to the next block, at least, I
Think I'll think of it, when these streets release
Me a scent, rotten as summer—a sight
As gray as blue. I'll say hello when I
See you. This is what to do with the dead.
Tell them, your mountains are grand as breezes.
You can hear. And you can see, shimmering,
Your tableware patterns of luscious fruit.
It feels fresh at this depth, underground, where
You keep everything I say in season.

(XXIII)

And the way some green is turning greener,
Summer is mad. It is very mad. It
Fills with days, green days filled with green branches,
Green assortments. With enough. Green enough
To wake up in the yard, verdant, fresh,
Halfway through a memory, straight as rain,
Falling asleep in my chair, driving,
Everywhere, my eyes heave to be open.
It is heavy to be in the summer
Now. The summer always almost over.
To stand, to strain, to start to speak. To end
On here a list as fragrant as the heat.
To sit alone, thick as an urn, mad, mad
Enough to spell each word its own green turn.

(XXIV)

The minutes were hastening. It was three,
And people were trying more actively
To kill the university at noon
That day, while the professors were asleep,
Reading to themselves, in July's glow, in
Summer cotton. They were the rind on some
Beautiful fruit, being pulled off and tossed,
Layers there less them more they ate and ate.
It was noon again, then four. They read with
Concern for that which goes before. They read
As clouds passed over their book, and when it
Was time for the rains to come at five,
They read themselves out of the day—too late,
The sun came back to come back in a rage.

(XXV)

Summer is never over. The winds dance.
Office buildings collapse in the weather.
I walk around them, their glass, little heaps
Shake in place in the breeze. Like they're alive.
I stride by. I see grasses, branches, trees.
The greens in my eye verge so suddenly
They fade—but strange, like a match that's burning
Without the flame. A lawn drawn out as ghosts
Of a lawn. A mood I can't get over.
There's only more. Block after block, it's not
The heat in the street, but something running
Alongside that feels the same—if I take
A shower, or if I take a plane—it
Doesn't come off me, and I don't complain.

(XXVI)

Things feel lost. The waves rush from their centers.
Distantly, a container is loaded
And brought to port, and I can't see the port
Where the containers are stacked, nor those things
Inside them, some of which belong to me.
The winds shift in the branches, revealing
Inside the shadow I have been watching
Is nothing, no bird, no nest. I think now
It's hard to say when the storm has ended,
If you watch the waves seem to settle, still,
Then they swell again. Beach grass rifles
At the edge of my shape. Air near the clouds
Takes on a color I don't understand.
I'll head back now, as if that was the plan.

(XXVII)

I stand in the surf with Eddie Vedder.
We are apart together, here, the end
Of summer, our goblets almost all but
In the white water, as it rolls in, wave
After wave, like the darkness around us.
This evening now comes, has come, and is
What's coming. Shadow or wave. I don't know
How to tell which is more upon us, so
Eddie, I say, let's get into the thing.
Let's throw our voices out to sea, listen
For what rides back, for what we can hear of
This arc we occupy for however
Long before it recedes, complete and known.
The one clear, cold air we breathe in alone.

(XXVIII)

The seasons are here, and the seasons I
Encounter, walking to my car, arms filled
With plastic, while little mechanical
Sounds spill on the ground before my feet, while
Fruit is purchased—by me—and dropped around
The yard as I eat. Orange berries pear.
Treats I grind in my teeth while waiting for
The bright work to begin. I read a bit.
The seasons are my fortune, and they spill on
My feet like fruit I buy and never eat.
I read up about seasons, the seasons' plans
I keep, as I roll around in my yard
Breathing breaths in places until I feel
Warm and numb. I am nothing like the sun.

/ // /// //// /////

(XXIX)

I feel mellow, welcome, full of mist as
Morning rolls its seasons through town, block on
Block opening almost a chill the air
Lays on my skin. Something I wear like yes,
We're in balance: a muscle in my sleeve,
A breath in my breast, a book in my bag,
A thought in my text, one that knows my name,
What speed I go when I read, when I drive
Late in the night, when I find I'm alive—
I lose the sentence, when I don't want to
Go home. I'm out at the diner, a cough
In the cold. This is a place that doesn't
Close. It's morning at night. I'm here. I'm here.
I'll talk all day until I disappear.

(XXX)

I walk past the house where I used to live,
While I used to live there, that is the way
The wind sweeps leafless air past me as I
Can't get back to my business, moving me
Where I went there, I went there, and the wind
Brought on the fall in me, from my window,
Watching carefully as I walked there, where
I made myself fall from the window, where,
As I fell, I could not keep from watching
Myself turn brown to blue, all afternoon,
While half my vision got roughed up, obscure
As a cloud front taking half the sky, one
I approach as wind moving in the branches,
Searching my hands for what the storm passes.

(XXXI)

On the university campus, leaves
Leave branches out where I might see them, where
They go galloping in circles where there
Is water and where there is dirt. I doubt
I'm going to get done with everything.
In a line or on a curve, settling
In place or getting going again, sun
Setting silver fevers in my fingers,
Nonsense I like but can't feel. Nothing feels
In its place. Nothing stays. The years come up
On me through my scalp and then they heave down.
They want me to hold them with me as I
Walk and pace, as a cafeteria
Window appears last to adjust my smile.

(XXXII)

This is the season I decide to be
Calm. To live, calmly, by the stacks of wood,
With the front door open, the storm door shut,
With my face under a book, soft and firm,
Or in my green car, in the dirt drive, out
To cool winds, making spaces in the air.
I do my work, come home, thinking nothing
Of it. There's the one day, then the next day,
I'm parked in the car, before the woodpile,
Listening to an album I can't tell
From what I remember which one, I think
It's raining so hard I can't get inside,
Or it may have been so clear it hurts to
Build, from the thought of it, my cold purpose.

(XXXIII)

I feel full of speech, lightly—a lightness
In what I say, as I walk on the streets,
As I climb in the trees. So, once again,
It's the fall, and every morning is bright
As time passing, time familiar as here,
Now, where I sit on a wide porch railing,
Looking at my knee, contemplatively.
Take a picture of me. Before I change
Position. Position myself so that
I see there are things I want to pursue,
Wants I want to do. I don't like to know
What I'm after until I'm through. The trees
Fill with hours that tower in the winds, while
The street holds each minute so still it ends.

(XXXIV)

Everyone with their faces getting
Older, and I can't choose which I like less,
Money or death, as the sky turns blue turns
Gray, another day pours its tender shapes
Around me. The patch of grass I lie on
Is warm, and I feel a little like my lips
Open. I stand myself at the end of
A long stone walkway in a photograph,
Except I can't keep still, I'm wavering.
First, I let my neck fall out of my coat,
Then I'm naked, and little black flashes
Cover the film or frame of whatever
Part of me I'm trying to see. Laid flat
In bed, I can't tell if I'm rich or dead.

(XXXVI)

The world is charged with faces bright as wings
On a bird lifting to a street sign, while
Fresh screams of I don't know when to do what
Are where I can't locate them with my eyes.
This is when I went to soil where I sat.
Eastward streamed petals I happened to have
Sat among or trod where my foot could feel
Could feel could feel for how my foot's been spent.
The world is well, and I look for a point
I make, the one I explain when I do
What when I do what when I thought I was
Expected to. I try to but to find
A mirror in my place. I'm very fine.
The world is full of light and full of grace.

(XXXVII)

I watch the news as it comes, a sentence
Getting its green letters and numbers in
Me. I'd rather be with my friends, driving,
We're 17, holding our newports in
The wind. Everyone has a sweatshirt.
Everyone has a gray tee. At dawn,
Blue newspapers arrive on all the lawns.
Each like a width bending in my fingers.
What does this sentence say I ask myself
As I say it here and feel like I'm in
A river, jeans in the water, hands in
My pockets. You think words'll escape you,
And then you find they won't release. I see
Whatever was is lost, but not from me.

(XXXVIII)

Lots of different places quietly dead.
Autumnal, I put my foot down to it.
Orange color, brown color, red, yellow,
I saw, afterward, on a telephone
Call full of feelings, indivisible
Feelings, feelings full and cold and cloaked in
Windshields, license plates, tire piles. Then the sound
When the door opens I come to count on.
I hide my feelings in the future but
They come right back to me. Here, a turn
In the memory, whatever memory
I slide past it now, past flagstone, piling
This up faster than I can leave my head,
Where the yards were green, and the street set in.

(XXXIX)

The street I read this book on it in bed
Asleep. I went along a TV street,
Then a red street, then a street alongside
A river, where I woke as asphalt fell
About my head. You should be dead, I said.
I'm up and out of town. Not everything
Fits, that's the story. It's majestic in
The moments before the election, but
If the hour falls, if the street is cleared
Or filled, if I forget in the midst of
A sentence what I was going to say,
If the sea is silent, if I see it,
If I've read about it, if it comes on
Shore. If I heard a rumor once before.

(XL)

Out in the bitter blue, the vacant street,
The night, as it filled in with news of what
We'd known as we slept, now written out as
A fact we met, we meet still. As I went
With Lizzie through the day, passing between
Supermarket strangers—one two three—there
As if nothing had occurred, as if one
Couldn't taste the actual fires burning
Tennessee. I don't know how to turn back
To my mouth hanging tears through the doorway,
Held there, hiding from my kid what fear is
As I'm not afraid now. I've been swiftly
Remade. I can touch fingers to my face
And when I look, nothing is out of place.

(XLI)

The forest was green and white. It filtered
Light. It held a coolness like a path through
The woods, or rather, it was cool along
The path between the trees, over where trees
Had fallen, where there were other shades of
Brown and black and green. A light on the trunk
Of what was left of a tree came down out
The branches between green-white leaves. It was
Green, white. Then there was very little light.
A foot could be put firmly to the earth.
To the dirt. The pieces of trees that fell
Had changed after falling, broken beyond
Form. It had been cool in these trees, but now
The forest turned cold, colorless, vast, closed.

(XLII)

In my yard, I can fill up red things with
Air, my air, out of my own lungs, and since
There's no help, when I fill them up, the air
Can turn inside them so they grow more red
And more full in the light that's there. And since
There's no help, I can say whatever I
Like, and I can hear whatever I've said,
Like here, where I can sit and listen as
I say, since there's no help, it's fine. It's done.
I hear a hammer strike, but I don't see
Where the sound comes from. It turns like something
I've said before slips trouble in
My eye, and trouble in my view. I see
Now how what turns I've made turn in me too.

/ // /// //// /////

(XLIII)

A wind picked up. It wasn't a signal
Bright in some silver night. It was morning.
It was the day someone died, and I was
Reading about them on my porch, and as
I read, I heard the wind pass through my most
Menacing patch of grass. I felt alone,
But I wasn't. People took to porches
To watch the sky fill with smoke and laughter.
Then it was endless night. Black SUVs
Rolled down my street, each filled with glowing meat.
I saw a pile of tires in a violet fire.
I saw a sewer flash with awful
Light. I turned from the world. I was in bed.
What put me in didn't come from my head.

(XLIV)

I knew my thoughts but was interested
In those I didn't know, thoughts gotten lost,
Like my voice, which I pursued in a park's
Dark thicket bending branches. It echoed,
Opening where I hadn't planned, as if
I planned a meadow, where I might grow cold,
And in my weather, head home with a chill
Held close, feeling between in me to say
He who wants my thought, I put him out of
Doubt. As well as I may as night comes on.
As well as I may while the light's yet there.
As well as I may in the evening air,
Watch it with me, here, when a shadow's cut,
It falls apart, though it may seem enough.

(XLV)

I woke in a tree's hard bark black copper.
My senses settled over things. I saw
Dogs yelping in the neighbor's property
Take me in their eyes, their eyes wet like leaves
In the darkness, not streetlamps nor moonlight
On branches I could see thinking. I could
Not resist the thought my sheets could hold warm
My body, then twitched another darkness.
It was very cold. I had fallen on
The ice trying to kick a car mirror
Off the car where I planned to park, angry
I picked my body up, and kicked again,
While I watched the memory grow colder
Around me, I breathed bright black as it bloomed.

(XLVI)

I had a lot of things I had to do.
I read aloud. I walked and checked and walked
Further in my yard, farther where the wind
Goes through the big tree like a horse breaking
Free, and my desire to keep pace with it
Kept me with it as far as the corner
Where there was no sun in the sky, and no
End to the street. My work wouldn't complete.
The horse was a fiction I made myself
An image of. I wasn't someone else.
I was no one, what that could be. I moved
My fingers out of time. I worked for where
I found I was, somewhere in an absence,
Like an owl at noon, staring from a fence.

(XLVII)

I think it cold in the hole where I feel
Blue, or a bluish gray; I feel violet,
Like in a painting of one, more violets
Pile around it high as I put an eye
To my window screen, feeling my teeth. I
Know my body, all its parts, my pink mouth
Opens as day churns through itself my yard.
I keep an eye on the time around me,
And then, I feel afraid with my legs out
Under my desk, hung there in a pool of
Possibilities. Outside, branches clear
The light away. I breathe colorlessly,
Letting skies weld their pinks to reds; leaving
My glasses the dresser, I warm the bed.

(XLVIII)

I forget like this. I pick a thing up
Like I put a thing down. Someone asks me
For something in the other room, and I
Come back, forgetting myself, forgetting
My age, my temperament, the way I sit on
A couch with my feet in boots, barefoot, in
Shoes. I wake up like I forgot a pair
Of sneakers out in the dew, brush a pile
Of photographs off of me. I'm in one
At once, the living room light on my black
Leather jacket, a futon, a forty.
This is where I hold a thing in my hand.
I know I'm leaving I haven't yet, how
I see my place. I'm as young as my face.

(XLIX)

And all my pleasures are like yesterday.
And all what I see hardens in my past.
In the end, I don't know what to believe,
And I believe what I don't know this way.
I take things without meaning to and fit
Them into that part of me I can't let
Alone. Into the telephone I can
Be another of these people without
End. Memory answers me the most things.
I stand on the edge of my property,
Holding color on the brick and blue green.
A conversation stays. Endings are when
I want a feeling full, late, while a door
Presents me with the middle of the day.

(XXXV)

Here's a story I tell when my wind voice
Rains, when death lingering in the flower
Bush scents a cocktail I like on the plane.
If you listen and you know me, how I
Circle and hum, what I say, the sentence
It is words over and over holding
Corners of an order, from the curve of
The stairwell to the part I'm hunting for.
That's a story I'd tell if my rain voice
Would run, if I could take myself outside
And turn the sound loud, so the hills echoed
Gold and cold, past the grass dying in rows,
Where my voice would grow, brightly in a way
That catches me no matter what I say.

(L)

I put it together, while the wind turns
On the neighborhood, grasses and houses,
Long blocks of walls and rectangles, corner
On corner. Oh it piles up. Like a year.
I can't contain it inside my voice, held
There a whisper. There a whisper gets gone.
The neighborhood is gray and the wind is
Fading. I can't do anything with it.
A warning I hear but can't find again.
Some types of trees, overgrown, wildly
On the edge of the lawns. I am absent.
I have made room. I can take something in.
Now the change feels like it'll happen here.
The lights go out. I'm still chasing a deer.

(LI)

Like nothing, I stand in a gentle breeze,
On my porch, on that verge of brick and grass
Beside the road, out alone on stones of
A walkway under elegant branches
In my mind. I'm always walking in wind,
Talking to my friends, their voices the same
Though their cities change with how often I can
Find them. I'm always looking. I'm lonely.
There is the part of me that remembers,
And the part that tells the wind to go. Winds
I could tell they were all coming at once.
That's not how I want to listen. To be
Heard, as I start my story from where, what.
The light in the windows a blue-white cut.

(LII)

Phone calls piled up on my face, like a twitch,
A person I didn't know what to do
With myself, on the steps, paging my hand
Through a newspaper, unread. A story
The winter brings direction to a fire.
I held my arms, like sweetly, and when things
Fell from the trees, I picked them up, made neat
Piles, clear and clean, the opposite of what
I'd seen glitter in the night, narrative
Arrangements took my word, like a paper
Airplane, holding a detail in its curve.
That didn't make it acceptable, how
The world filled up with cold gray terms. A blur,
The lengths each day told me, and no house burned.

(LIII)

No one is here with me. I'm in a shape.
Light flickers in the grass words. There are sounds
Flying themselves in the wind, and when I
Touch them, they become cool, rectangular,
Blue air. This is an airfield, guitar-like
When I sit my fingers on the curve of
A branch to find it feels like bone. I put
A skull together and take my turn in
The face of the wind. It's rich out here where
An era eats a path through the grass. It's
Awful, unalterable, full of loss.
It's coming. It's what I don't know what it is.
It's the end of an hour. The grass turns,
White in the trees, the sky, a sheet of light.

(LIV)

Between the trees, the sky twisted the rain
Loose over interstate traffic, fierce, high,
Ridged with lightning, caught in it, hungover,
A friend dead, learning to drive to cities
And find my way home. I find my way home,
Blue sky, green leaves, a scene I know I knew
From the past, memory catching itself
Out on that edge, where it keeps coming through
A tree in a storm, up close, and then, far,
I couldn't find a cab, and the trains were
Frozen in place until someone nudged me
In the back seat, their car, out in the dirt
Where it's dark, cold, fires burn off in the sky,
Twisted distant, and my hand on the road.

(LV)

Winter's last incline gets lost in mountain,
Mountain, field, and floor. Single floor, single-
Family houses, the edge of a pile
Of green coats, polyester as wool, then
Sunglass racks, seemingly out of sync with
The salt crystals, their crush, supermarket
Cake toppers, mud mats, automatic doors
Opening on the day, opening like
High school circles, scheduled to the eyes,
Drifts in the middle of what had to be
Warm, warmed over, without success. It falls,
The shine on the water boulders, new spans
I never put my hands to. Give in,
Rattling through the end, on the bridge winds.

(LVI)

I took a look in the rain window, iced-
Over maps on the wall, felt it drift past
A line, drawings of a tree, lake water
Where everything thins, maybe a store
Opposite a gray opening, it, flat,
A paper take on a city. It was
Where an awning had settled into place
Over several decades, tin and still,
I don't know what comes after all of it.
I'm stopped in a silver supermarket
Plaza, stepping out of my car, crowded
With ghost lines, carts, sounds, it's moving closer
While it swallows it up, growing with it
When I cut the air, northern, gray, severe.

/ // /// //// /////

(LVII)

Divers out in the seasonless movements,
Abandoned like houses, piling the dust
Tented over yards and parkways, places
And sentences we found our way into
How they catch, so different, the light, each, now,
As they fall, it gets dim, an open mouth
Holding a song wide and violet, like
A crossbeam lifts us as long as we leave.
Divers, the day is over, look, now, one
Way is headed toward another, where we live
In view of trees, branches we may lift our
Bodies into, ourselves, those falling from
The trees around us, look, how we fall down,
Up there, past our eyes, and out of bounds.

(LVIII)

The divers find a detail in the sky.
It's nothing they like. It starts the day off
Wrong, rolls the ground out around them, hot as
A still tongue. A cat's tongue. A tongue that speaks
Something in the day of the neighborhood,
Where they breathe it in, unfit, wrestling
Down sounds this news pours out. I can't stand it.
No one can. It blisters, spits in one's ears.
It's heard. It's spoken of, so much it drives
The divers to climb up onto porch roofs,
Water towers, industrial fencing,
Wires, lines, cables, places where no foot can
Hold. Everyone knows this is the end of
The show. We close our mouths, and then we go.

(LIX)

It's a dim hour, as the air waves off,
As divers recede in windows, faces
Turning to papers, texts rising after
The day is over. The day turns over.
No one remembers it. It pixelates,
Colored squares trading places in a field.
The divers fall into their couches, backward
On their beds, their necks bulging up
Beautifully. The day is never over.
That's how they say it—someone notices
A silence or a hum—it's in their house,
They look for it, they listen, they sit there
As if they're going to stand, rise, until
They feel like they're falling backward, inside.

(LX)

I see myself minutely, in situ,
Searching the sky as I plummet, and clouds
Catch across my torso, as I escape
And stray, contemplating how it went down
This way. My day over like a basement
Door. I've found my body in a place like
This before. An orange glow to those words,
Hazy as furniture I don't know how
Is here. I sit on one table, late in
The sun. My breath cool as a molecule.
It makes blue divers run across my veins.
I sing with them until the song is done.
Yesterday, tomorrow I would embrace,
And fall away while falling into place.

Acknowledgments

Gratitude to the editors of journals where poems from this collection previously appeared: *American Poetry Review, Bennington Review, Copper Nickel, Denver Quarterly, Fence, The Georgia Review, Harpur Palate, The Iowa Review, The Journal, The Kenyon Review, Laurel Review, The Minnesota Review, Mississippi Review, North Dakota Quarterly, Plume, Prelude, Touch the Donkey, The Volta, Volt.*

The majority of this book was written between 2016 and 2022. I am grateful to the friends, colleagues, students, and family who were a part of my life in different ways during those variously difficult and wonderful years, and I am thankful to the friends who read these poems in manuscript, especially Liz Countryman, Joshua Edwards, and Eric Kocher. I am appreciative to the University of South Carolina for supporting this book project with an Excel grant as well as a McCausland College of Arts & Sciences Book Manuscript Finalization Support Initiative award.

These sonnets were written while reading sonnets, many sonnets, and they on occasion borrow a phrase or an image or a word or a line from sonnets and other poems by John Ashbery, Ted Berrigan, Lucie Brock-Broido, John Donne, Michael Drayton, Gerard Manley Hopkins, John Keats, John Milton, Philip Sidney, Wallace Stevens, William Shakespeare, William Wordsworth, and Thomas Wyatt. I am further indebted to the sonnets of the many authors I read frequently but did not borrow from, including John Clare, Wanda Coleman, Edwin Denby, Terrance Hayes, Lyn Hejinian, Stéphane Mallarmé, Bernadette Mayer, Marianne Moore, Evie Shockley, Charlotte Smith, and Karen Volkman among many others.

Samuel Amadon is the author of five books of poetry, including *Listener* and *Often, Common, Some, And Free*. His poems have appeared in *The New Yorker*, *The Nation*, *Lana Turner*, *Volt*, *Fence*, and elsewhere. He teaches in the MFA Program at the University of South Carolina, where, with Liz Countryman, he edits the journal *Oversound*.

DIVERS

by Samuel Amadon

Cover art: "Batterman Dives (Multiflash), 1955" © Harold Edgerton/MIT, courtesy Palm Press, Inc.

Cover typeface: Abril Fatface

Interior design by Laura Joakimson

Interior typeface: Garamond Premier Pro

Printed in the United States by Books International, Dulles, Virginia on Acid Free Archival Quality Recycled Paper

Publication of this book was made possible in part by gifts from Katherine & John Gravendyk in honor of Hillary Gravendyk, Francesca Bell, Mary Mackey, and The New Place Fund

Omnidawn Publishing

Oakland, California